THE BATHROOM BASEBALL BOOK

by

Jack Kreismer

RED-LETTER PRESS, INC.
Saddle River, New Jersey

For information address:

Red-Letter Press, Inc.
P.O. Box 393, Saddle River, NJ 07458
www.Red-LetterPress.com

ACKNOWLEDGMENTS

Project Development Coordinator:
Kobus Reyneke

Cover design and typography:
s.w.artz, inc.

Editorial:
Jeff Kreismer

Significant Others:
Theresa Adragna
Kathy Hoyt, Robin Kreismer
Jim & Rory Tomlinson, Lori Walsh

INTRODUCTION

For more than twenty years, the original Bathroom Library has entertained people "on the go" everywhere.
With millions of copies out there, it proves that we're not all wet about bathroom reading.

Now, as heir to the throne, we proudly introduce a brand new Bathroom Library. We hope you enjoy this installment of it.

Yours flushingly,

Jack Kreismer
Publisher

FOR AMERICA'S
FAVORITE READING ROOM

THE BATHROOM BASEBALL BOOK

*Hardball Trivia for
The Best Seat
in The House*

THE BATHROOM LIBRARY

RED-LETTER PRESS, INC.
Saddle River, New Jersey

FIRST THINGS FIRST

1. In 1978, what Detroit Tiger became the first player to appear as a designated hitter in all 162 games?

2. Name the first man to play every position in a nine inning game.

3. Where was baseball's first night game played?

4. What team, since the inception of the American League in 1901, became the first club to switch leagues?

5. Who was the first player to win batting titles in three different decades?

6. Who was the first pro athlete to appear on the front of a Wheaties box?

7. Do you know the player who hit the first walk-off home run in history to win the World Series?

8. Who was the first man to hit 50 or more home runs in four consecutive seasons?

9. Who's the first player to hit three homers in a game three times in the same season?

10. In which World Series was the first game played in a domed stadium?

ANSWERS

1. Rusty Staub.

2. Bert Campaneris.

3. At Crosley Field in Cincinnati on May 24, 1935.

4. The Milwaukee Brewers ... They moved from the AL Central to the NL Central in 1998.

5. George Brett, in the '70s, '80s and '90s.

6. Pete Rose, 1985.

7. Bill Mazeroski, for the Pirates against the Yankees in 1960.

8. Mark McGwire.

9. Sammy Sosa, in 2001.

10. 1987, when the Cardinals played the Twins at Minnesota's Metrodome.

INFIELD CHATTER

"You never know with those psychosomatic injuries.
You have to take your time with them."

-Jim Palmer

CURVEBALLS

1. Who was the first African-American 20- game winner in the big leagues?

2. What hurler holds the record for most games started in a World Series?

3. Who was drafted by the National Hockey League's Los Angeles Kings in 1984 but wound up on another playing field with the Atlanta Braves?

4. He pitched in the big leagues from 1963-89, missing 1975 due to arm surgery after which he said, "I asked the doctors to give me Koufax's arm. They did ... Mrs. Koufax's." Name him.

5. Who threw the pitch that Hank Aaron hit for home run number 715?

6. Can you name the pitchers who threw a perfect game in back-to-back years for the Yankees?

7. What pitcher holds the record for most Gold Gloves?

8. Who's lost the most games in major league history?

9. Do you know the first pitcher to win at least one game against every present-day team?

10. Who's thrown the most career no-hitters?

ANSWERS

1. Don Newcombe of the Brooklyn Dodgers, 20-9, in 1951.

2. Whitey Ford, 22.

3. Tom Glavine.

4. Tommy John.

5. Al Downing.

6. David Wells and David Cone, in 1998 and 1999.

7. Jim Kaat, 16.

8. Cy Young ... He's also won the most (511-315).

9. Al Leiter.

10. Nolan Ryan, seven.

INFIELD CHATTER

"Baseball is pitching, fundamentals and three-run homers."

-Earl Weaver

PLAYING BY THE RULES

1. A runner standing on third base is hit by a line drive. Is the runner safe or out?

2. True or false? The maximum allowable length of a bat is 48 inches.

3. The first baseman stumbles and loses his glove. While lying on his stomach, he reaches out and makes the catch with his hat. Is this allowed?

4. A line drive hits the pitcher's mound and ricochets into the first base dugout. What's the call?

5. Barry Bonds hits one out of the park, but the umpire notices that his back foot was on the back line of the batter's box. Is it still a home run?

6. Is it legal to hit a pitch that bounces before the plate?

7. How many of the bases are in fair territory?

8. What's the score of a forfeited game?

9. Is a batter awarded first base if a pitch bounces and then hits him?

10. In this hypothetical situation, Ken Griffey Jr. goes back for a deep fly ball. The ball bounces off the wall, hits Griffey on his forehead and then rebounds over the wall. What's the call?

ANSWERS

1. Out.

2. False ... It's 42 inches.

3. No ... It's a three base penalty for illegal use of equipment.

4. Foul ball.

5. Yes.

6. Yes.

7. All four.

8. 9-0.

9. Yes.

10. It's a ground rule double.

INFIELD CHATTER

"I believe we owe something to the people who watch us.
They work hard for their money. When we do not try one
hundred per cent, we steal from them."

-*Roberto Clemente*

WHO AM I?

1. I played in 14 World Series games (seven in 1960 and seven in 1971) and hit safely in every one of them. (Hint: In my career, I had exactly 3,000 hits.)

2. I was the cover boy for the very first edition of *Sports Illustrated* in 1954.

3. I played more years than anyone else in big league history.

4. My 3,000th hit was a home run.

5. I was the beer-drinking coach of *The Bad News Bears* Little League team.

6. I was the first slugger with over 400 career homers to not be elected to the Hall of Fame when I became eligible.

7. I hold baseball's career stolen base record.

8. We are the only two people in the Baseball Hall of Fame who are not connected with the sport.

9. My real first name is George and I managed both an American League and a National League World Series winner.

10. I was the first player ever to hit 50 homers and 50 doubles in the same season.

ANSWERS

1. Roberto Clemente.

2. Eddie Mathews.

3. Nolan Ryan.

4. Wade Boggs.

5. Walter Matthau.

6. Dave Kingman.

7. Rickey Henderson.

8. Abbott and Costello, for their *Who's on First?* routine.

9. Sparky Anderson.

10. Albert Belle.

INFIELD CHATTER

"Just give me 25 guys on the last year of their contract; I'll win a pennant every year."

-Sparky Anderson

NEVER-NEVER LAND

True or false ...

1. Willie Mays never hit a World Series home run.

2. Roger Maris was never intentionally walked when he hit 61 homers in 1961.

3. Stan Musial never stole a base.

4. The Montreal Expos never played in a World Series.

5. Michael Jordan never played in an official major league game.

6. Babe Ruth never played in a night game.

7. The Seattle Mariners have never retired a uniform number.

8. Mike Piazza never homered in an All-Star Game.

9. Joe DiMaggio never won an MVP award.

10. There has never been a major league umpire who wore glasses.

INFIELD CHATTER

"Half of Jeff King's extra-base hits last year were extra-base hits."

-Ralph Kiner

ANSWERS

1. True.

2. True.

3. False.

4. True.

5. True.

6. True.

7. True.

8. False.

9. False.

10. False ... The first to wear glasses was Ed Rommel in 1956.

INFIELD CHATTER

"The only thing running and exercising can do for you
is make you healthy."

-Mickey Lolich

TWO-FERS

1. Which two Yankees both homered, in the same game, from both sides of the plate in 2000, the first teammates to do so?

2. Of all the players whose last name begins with "T," which two have the most career home runs? (Hint: You'll be seeing double with this answer.)

3. In 1963, two Hall of Famers tied for the NL lead in home runs, hitting the same number as each wore on his uniform. Who are they? (Hint: Each has hit more than 500 home runs.)

4. From 1954 to 1996 the Dodgers had only two managers. Who were they?

5. There have been two pitchers who struck out as many batters in a big league game as their ages. Can you name them?

6. Do you know the two brothers who each had 21 victories in 1979 to lead the NL in wins?

7. Who were the last players to hit .400 in each league?

8. Name the two Heisman Trophy winners who have been major leaguers.

9. In what two cities did the Atlanta Braves previously play their home games?

10. Hall of Famers Paul and Lloyd Waner were known by what nicknames?

ANSWERS

1. Bernie Williams and Jorge Posada.

2. Frank Thomas (still playing) and Frank Thomas. The latter played for numerous National League clubs in the '50s and '60s, clubbing 286 home runs.

3. Hank Aaron and Willie McCovey.

4. Walter Alston and Tommy Lasorda.

5. Bob Feller, 17, and Kerry Wood, 20.

6. Joe and Phil Niekro.

7. Ted Williams (AL) and Bill Terry (NL).

8. Vic Janowicz and Bo Jackson.

9. Boston and Milwaukee.

10. Big Poison and Little Poison.

INFIELD CHATTER

"When I was a kid, I practiced eight hours a day for nothing, so why shouldn't I do the same when I got to be a pro?"

-Hank Greenberg

FIELDS OF DREAMS

1. What was San Diego's Qualcomm Stadium formerly called?

2. Where did the Toronto Blue Jays play their home games before the Skydome opened?

3. What was the first home of the New York Mets?

4. True or false? The Anaheim Angels played their initial year at Wrigley Field.

5. This ballpark was the home field for both of the World Series participants in 1944. Can you name it?

6. Do you have any idea how tall Fenway's Green Monster is?

7. The San Francisco Giants play at Pacific Bell Park. Before that, they played at 3Com Park (formerly Candlestick). Where did they play before that?

8. What was Atlanta's Turner Field originally called?

9. What's baseball's oldest stadium?

10. In what year was the first night game played at Chicago's Wrigley Field?

ANSWERS

1. Jack Murphy Stadium.

2. Exhibition Stadium.

3. The Polo Grounds.

4. True ... In 1961 the Angels played at Wrigley, a longtime minor league ballpark in Los Angeles.

5. Sportsman's Park in St. Louis where the Cardinals beat the Browns, four games to two.

6. 37 feet.

7. Seals Stadium.

8. Centennial Olympic Stadium.

9. Fenway Park which opened in 1912.

10. 1988.

INFIELD CHATTER

"They give you a round bat and they throw you a round ball. And they tell you to hit it square."

- Willie Stargell

SCREEN TEST

1. Who's the creator of the critically acclaimed PBS television series documentary *Baseball*?

2. *Fear Strikes Out* was a film about what zany baseball player of the '50s and '60s?

3. What character did Robert Redford portray in *The Natural*?

4. Who played Hall of Famer Grover Cleveland Alexander in *The Winning Team*?

5. Name the 1994 family flick that had parts for Leon Durham, Kevin Elster, Don Mattingly, Ken Griffey Jr. and Jason Robards Jr.

6. Who played The Babe in *The Babe Ruth Story*?

7. What 1988 comedy featured Reggie Jackson, Jay Johnstone, Jim Palmer, Tim McCarver and Leslie Nielsen?

8. Who portrayed Jackie Robinson in *The Jackie Robinson Story*?

9. Who played a catcher dying of Hodgkin's disease in *Bang the Drum Slowly*?

10. Charlie Sheen, Bob Uecker and Tom Berenger starred in what movie about a lovable band of misfits and loonies who turn around the fate of the hapless Cleveland Indians?

ANSWERS

1. Ken Burns.

2. Jimmy Piersall.

3. Roy Hobbs.

4. Ronald Reagan.

5. *Little Big League.*

6. There were three films about the Babe - William Bendix, Stephen Lang and John Goodman each portrayed him.

7. *Naked Gun.*

8. Robinson played himself.

9. Robert DeNiro.

10. *Major League.*

INFIELD CHATTER

"How hard is hitting? You ever walk into a pitch-black room full of furniture that you've never been in before and try to walk through it without bumping into anything? Well, it's harder than that."

- Ted Kluszewski

THREE ON A MATCH

1. Do you know the three brothers who played in the same outfield in the same game for the San Francisco Giants on September 15, 1963?

2. During his 56 game hitting streak in 1941, Joe DiMaggio coincidentally had two other "56" categories. What were they?

3. Who, in 1905, hurled three shutouts in the World Series?

4. Can you name three current baseball stadiums which have hosted both a World Series and a Super Bowl?

5. Name the only three players to play 1,000 games in both the National and American Leagues.

6. Despite never moving more than a county away, the Angels have used three different geographical names. What are they?

7. Three men who hit 40 or more homers in a season had brothers who also played in the big leagues. Can you name them?

8. What three Hall of Famers played during the 1970's and never spent a day in the minor leagues?

9. Three players who have logged at least 1,000 big league games sport a career average of .350 or better. How many do you know?

10. What were the distances to the right, center and left field fence in Yankee Stadium before it was renovated?

ANSWERS

1. The Alous - Felipe, Matty and Jesus.

2. He also had 56 singles and 56 runs during the streak.

3. Christy Mathewson, for the New York Giants against the Philadelphia Athletics.

4. Miami's Pro Player Stadium, Qualcomm Stadium in San Diego and the Metrodome in Minneapolis. (The Memorial Coliseum in Los Angeles, where the Dodgers played for their first three years, also hosted a World Series and a Super Bowl.)

5. Bob Boone, Frank Robinson and Dave Winfield.

6. The Los Angeles Angels, California Angels and Anaheim Angels (present).

7. Hank Aaron (brother Tommie), Joe DiMaggio (Dom and Vince) and Richie Allen (Hank and Ron).

8. Ernie Banks, Catfish Hunter and Al Kaline.

9. Ty Cobb (.367), Rogers Hornsby (.358) and Shoeless Joe Jackson (.356).

10. 296 feet to right, 461 to center and 301 to left.

FOUR-LETTER WORDS

The answers to these all have four-letter last names.

1. Can you name the tennis great whose brother, Randy Moffit, pitched for the Giants in the '70s?

2. Babe Ruth hit his "called" shot in the 1932 World Series off what Cubs pitcher?

3. Who was the first African-American player in the American League?

4. At the age of 22 in 1971, this switch-hitter was the youngest ever to win the MVP award. Who is he?

5. Who has more at-bats than anyone in big league history?

6. Do you know the Pirates reliever who had an 18-1 record in 1959?

7. Who had a career pitching record of 94-46, mostly as a moundsman for the Red Sox?

8. What pitcher won the most World Series games?

9. With 524 lifetime homers, he's fifth among all American Leaguers. Can you name him?

10. Who's caught the most games ever?

ANSWERS

1. Billie Jean King.

2. Charlie Root.

3. Larry Doby.

4. A's pitcher Vida Blue.

5. Pete Rose, 14,053.

6. Roy Face.

7. Babe Ruth.

8. Whitey Ford, ten.

9. Jimmie Foxx.

10. Carlton Fisk.

INFIELD CHATTER

"I swing big, with everything I've got.
I hit big or I miss big. I like to live as big as I can."

-Babe Ruth

KEEPING SCORE

In this quiz, you're provided the date and the score.
Your job is to come up with the player who made the game eventful.

1. April 15, 1947 - Dodgers 5, Braves 3

2. September 6, 1995 - Orioles 4, Angels 2

3. May 2, 1939 - Yankees 22, Tigers 2

4. June 15, 1938 - Reds 6, Dodgers 0

5. September 30, 1927 - Yankees 4, Senators 2

6. October 3, 1951 - Giants 5, Dodgers 4

7. October 8, 1956 - Yankees 2, Dodgers 0

8. October 13, 1960 - Pirates 10, Yankees 9

9. October 21, 1975 - Red Sox 7, Reds 6 in 12 innings

10. October 23, 1993 - Blue Jays 8, Phillies 6

INFIELD CHATTER

"Baseball is a kid's game
that grownups only tend to screw up."

-Bob Lemon

ANSWERS

1. Jackie Robinson broke baseball's color barrier when he made his big league debut. He went 0-3, but reached base on an error in the seventh inning and came around to score the winning run.

2. Cal Ripken played in his 2,131st consecutive game to pass Lou Gehrig on the all-time iron-man list.

3. Lou Gehrig's 2,130 consecutive game streak ended.

4. Johnny Vander Meer threw his second consecutive no-hitter.

5. Babe Ruth hit his 60th homer.

6. Bobby Thomson hit the "shot heard 'round the world" to give the Giants a pennant-winning victory.

7. Don Larsen pitched a World Series perfect game.

8. Bill Mazeroski homered in the bottom of the ninth to clinch the Fall Classic for Pittsburgh.

9. Carlton Fisk hit a leadoff homer to give the Red Sox the World Series Game 6 win.

10. Joe Carter's three-run, ninth-inning home run enabled Toronto to win their second straight Series.

MIXING IT UP

So, now it's time for a word scramble. It's not a tremendously difficult task. All you have to do is come up with the initial letter from each sentence on this page. Mix the letters into the proper sequence and you'll have the answer to the following clues.

It was in the early sixties when this player hit his hundredth home run. Lo and behold what he did to celebrate! Everyone had an opinion about it. Many thought it was hilarious. Just as many thought it was insane. League officials were not at all amused. Rather than have this sort of thing happen again, the next day they issued a new rule. Players were no longer allowed to celebrate home runs in this fashion. You see, to commemorate his benchmark homer, this outfielder ran the bases backwards.

— — — — —   — — — — — — —

INFIELD CHATTER

"Baseball is like church. Many attend, but few understand."

- Wes Westrum

ANSWER

Jimmy Piersall.

Bonus question: What pitcher gave up Piersall's 100th homer? Hint: He was a reliever with the Phillies in the '60s and managed the 1980 Philadelphia club to a world championship.

(answer below)

Dallas Green.

INFIELD CHATTER

"I was in Little League. I was on first base - I stole third. I ran straight across the diamond. Earlier in the week, I learned the shortest distance between two points is a straight line. I argued with the ump that second base was out of my way."

-Comedian *Steven Wright*

KIDSTUFF

1. How did Carl Stotz make a small name for himself?

2. How far apart are bases on a Little League diamond?

3. In what town is the Little League World Series played?

4. What's the name of the facility where the Little League World Series is held?

5. What flame-throwing phenom from Brooklyn was expelled from the Little League World Series in 2001 when it was discovered that he was overage?

6. What "first" did Joey Jay of the Cincinnati Reds achieve?

7. The first Little League World Series championship game to be televised live was in 1985 on what network?

8. In 1989, this Red Sox player became the first Little Leaguer to be enshrined in the Baseball Hall of Fame. Who is he?

9. Name the Oriole first baseman who was the first Little Leaguer to play in a big league World Series.

10. Who's the only sitting U.S. president to throw out the ceremonial first pitch in a Little League World Series championship game?

ANSWERS

1. He founded Little League Baseball.

2. 60 feet.

3. Williamsport, PA.

4. Howard J. Lamade Little League World Series Stadium.

5. Danny Almonte.

6. He was the first Little Leaguer to make it to the big leagues.

7. ABC, on Wide World of Sports.

8. Carl Yastrzemski.

9. Boog Powell.

10. George W. Bush.

INFIELD CHATTER

"A lot of people my age are dead at the present time."

-Casey Stengel

PHRASE CRAZE

See if you can figure out the baseball lingo these items represent.

1. Play
   Play
   Play

2. r
   e
   t
   t
   a
   B

3. Base
   Balls

4. Buc foot ket

5. e T
   e h
   r r
   h e
   T e

6. Header
   Header

7. hsurb

8. e
   g
   n
   a
   h
   C

9. pots

10. Sea/mer

ANSWERS

1. Triple play.

2. Batter up.

3. Base on balls.

4. Foot in the bucket.

5. Three up, three down.

6. Doubleheader.

7. Brushback.

8. Changeup.

9. Backstop.

10. Split seamer.

INFIELD CHATTER

"Fans don't boo nobodies."

-Reggie Jackson

A LEAGUE OF THEIR OWN

1. Nine members of the Baseball Hall of Fame played in both the Negro and the Major Leagues. How many do you know?

2. James Thomas Bell was one of the best and swiftest players in the Negro leagues, so quick that it was said he "could flip off the light and get into bed before the room got dark." By what paternally slick nickname was he known?

3. In 1988, the Baseball Hall of Fame opened a permanent exhibition called "Women in Baseball" to honor the AAGPBL. What does AAGPBL stand for?

4. The Senior Professional Baseball Association, a league set up to feature former big leaguers 35 and over, lasted just one full season. Where were its games played?

5. Where is the college World Series played?

6. The Richmond Braves, Columbus Clippers and Norfolk Tides are teams in what league?

7. Josh Gibson was the greatest home run hitter in Negro leagues history, believed to have hit 962 homers in his 17-year career. Can you name one of the two teams he played for?

8. What minor league distinction does Pam Postema hold?

9. Do you know the women's team that made its name by traveling around the country, primarily playing against men's amateur teams?

10. The longest game in organized baseball history was played between the Pawtucket Red Sox and Rochester Red Wings in 1981. How many innings did it go?

ANSWERS

1. Hank Aaron, Ernie Banks, Roy Campanella, Larry Doby, Monte Irvin, Willie Mays, Satchel Paige, Billy Williams and Jackie Robinson.

2. Cool Papa Bell.

3. All-American Girls Professional Baseball League, which featured women's teams from 1943 to 1954.

4. In Florida, from November 1, 1989, to February 4, 1990.

5. Omaha, Nebraska.

6. The AAA's International League.

7. The Homestead Grays and Pittsburgh Crawfords.

8. She was the first woman to umpire at the AAA level, in 1989.

9. The Colorado Silver Bullets.

10. 33.

INFIELD CHATTER

"I get up at 6 a.m. no matter what time it is."

-Yogi Berra

BASEBALL BAFFLERS

1. Name the U.S. Senator who pitched a perfect game.

2. Who's the only man to have two major league stadiums named after him?

3. In what offensive category is Tris Speaker the all-time leader with 792?

4. Three players have homered in a record eight consecutive games. How many do you know?

5. Who was the first player to be named Rookie of the Year and MVP in the same season?

6. How about the first pitcher to win the Cy Young Award and Rookie of the Year Award in the same year?

7. Who's the only player to hit two grand slams in the same inning?

8. Two players have won baseball's Triple Crown twice. Can you name either one?

9. Who won the 1994 World Series?

10. Cleveland Indian Hall of Famer Bob Feller once threw a no-hitter against Chicago, yet none of the White Sox' batting averages changed. How can that be?

ANSWERS

1. Jim Bunning, for the Phillies against the Mets in 1964.

2. Charles Comiskey - the old and new Comiskey Park.

3. Doubles.

4. Dale Long, Don Mattingly and Ken Griffey Jr.

5. Fred Lynn, of the Red Sox, in 1975.

6. Dodger pitcher Fernando Valenzuela, in 1981.

7. Fernando Tatis, of the Cardinals, in 1999.

8. Ted Williams and Rogers Hornsby.

9. No one ... It was cancelled due to the players' strike.

10. It was Opening Day (the only Opening Day no-hitter ever thrown).

INFIELD CHATTER

"I can remember a reporter asking for a quote,
and I didn't know what a quote was.
I thought it was some kind of soft drink."

-Joe DiMaggio

INITIALLY SPEAKING

*The number on the left is based upon the first letters
for the words on the right.*

1. 2,632 = C.G.P. by C.R.J.

2. 9 = I. in a B.G.

3. 755 = H.R. by H.A.

4. 162 = G. in a R.S.

5. 3 = S. and Y.O.

6. 42 = R.U.N. of J.R.

7. 6 = O. in an I.

8. 127', 3 3/8" = D. from H.P. to S.B.

9. 31 = G.W. by D.M. in 1968

10. 1/8 = U.N. of E.G.

INFIELD CHATTER

"I'm not a win-at-all-costs guy. Winning isn't everything.
It's second to breathing."

-George Steinbrenner

ANSWERS

1. 2,632 = Consecutive Games Played by Cal Ripken Jr.

2. 9 = Innings in a Baseball Game.

3. 755 = Home Runs by Hank Aaron.

4. 162 = Games in a Regular Season.

5. 3 = Strikes and You're Out.

6. 42 = Retired Uniform Number of Jackie Robinson.

7. 6 = Outs in an Inning.

8. 127', 3 3/8" = Distance from Home Plate to Second Base.

9. 31 = Games Won by Denny McLain in 1968.

10. 1/8 = Uniform Number of Eddie Gaedel ... The 3'7" Gaedel was sent up to the plate in a 1951 game as a promotional stunt by madcap St. Louis Browns owner Bill Veeck. Gaedel walked in his only appearance.

INFIELD CHATTER

"There is still nothing in life as constant and as changing at the same time as an afternoon at a ballpark."

-Larry King

ONE OR THE OTHER

1. Which is wider, home plate or first base?

2. Who was the first player to have his uniform retired, Ty Cobb or Lou Gehrig?

3. Were umpires once referred to as "Diamond Dicks" or "Blind Basemen?"

4. In 1998, Greg Vaughn and Mo Vaughn combined for 90 home runs, the most ever in a season by two players with the same last name. Who hit more, Greg or Mo?

5. What was the first expansion team to play in Canada, the Expos or Blue Jays?

6. Did Tom Seaver win his 300th game with the Mets or White Sox?

7. Was it Willie Nelson or Kenny Rogers who pitched a perfect game for the Rangers in 1994?

8. In the National League, what team has won the most World Series, the Cardinals or Dodgers?

9. Who has scored more runs, Rickey Henderson or Ty Cobb?

10. Who managed the most years in baseball history, Connie Mack or Casey Stengel?

ANSWERS

1. Home plate ... It's 17 inches wide while each of the bases are 15 inch squares.

2. Lou Gehrig.

3. "Diamond Dicks."

4. Greg hit 50, Mo 40.

5. The Expos, in 1969.

6. White Sox, in 1985.

7. Rogers.

8. The Cardinals, 9.

9. Rickey Henderson.

10. Connie Mack, 53 years.

INFIELD CHATTER

"Always go to other people's funerals. Otherwise they won't come to yours."

-Yogi Berra

LEFT-HANDED COMPLIMENTS

1. What southpaw threw a no-hitter in four consecutive seasons?

2. Who holds the record for most grand slams in a season?

3. What one-armed outfielder played for the St. Louis Browns of the American League in 1945?

4. What do Tony Kubek and Ted Williams have in common with home runs and Fenway Park?

5. What was the real first name of Hall of Famer Lefty Grove?

6. What colorful Red Sox lefthander was known as the "Spaceman?"

7. Name the pitcher who has the most lifetime victories for a lefthander.

8. What first baseman has won the most Gold Gloves?

9. Do you know the lefthanded batter who holds World Series records for most games played, most at-bats, hits, singles and doubles?

10. Who was the first designated hitter in baseball history?

ANSWERS

1. Sandy Koufax, for the Dodgers from 1962-65.

2. Don Mattingly, six, for the Yankees in 1987.

3. Lefthander Pete Gray.

4. Both lefthanded batters homered in their final major league at bat there.

5. Robert Grove.

6. Bill Lee.

7. Warren Spahn, 363.

8. Keith Hernandez, 11.

9. Yogi Berra.

10. Ron Blomberg.

INFIELD CHATTER

"I never questioned the integrity of an umpire.
Their eyesight, yes."

-*Leo Durocher*

COLOR MY WORLD

1. Who hit four home runs and garnered a record 19 total bases in a single game in 2002?

2. Eight members of the Chicago White Sox were banned from baseball for life for throwing the 1919 World Series against Cincinnati. What name was this incident given?

3. What nickname was Rusty Staub given when he played in Montreal?

4. What Gold-Glove winning first baseman became the president of the National League?

5. Who, in 1938, hit two home runs in the same game eleven times. Hint: He hit 58 dingers that season.

6. What team changed its name for a while during the cold war with Russia?

7. A Hall of Fame pitcher who won 239 games, you know Mordecai better by his nickname. What is it?

8. Can you name the first baseball player to also play in the Super Bowl?

9. John Odom had a 13 year career as a pitcher, mostly with the A's. Do you know his nickname?

10. After a 19 year career, what second baseman retired from the Cardinals in 1963 and later managed the club from 1965-'76?

ANSWERS

1. Shawn Green.

2. The Black Sox Scandal.

3. "Le Grand Orange."

4. Bill White.

5. Hank Greenberg.

6. The Cincinnati Reds (as in Soviets) changed their name to the Red Legs.

7. "Three Finger" Brown.

8. Tom Brown ... He played for the Washington Senators and the Green Bay Packers.

9. "Blue Moon."

10. Red Schoendienst.

INFIELD CHATTER

"Why does everyone stand up and sing
Take Me Out to the Ballgame when they're already there?"

-Larry Andersen

LAUGH-IN TIME-OUT

*It's time for a trivia breather
with these humorous one-liners from baseballers.*

"Winfield goes back to the wall. He hits his head on the wall, and it rolls off! It's rolling all the way back to second base! This is a terrible thing for the Padres!"
          -Padres play by play announcer Jerry Coleman

"We'll do all right if we can capitalize on our mistakes."
          -Yankees outfielder Mickey Rivers

"Mike Andrews' limitations are limitless."
          -Phillies manager Danny Ozark

"I found a delivery in my flaw."
          -Royals reliever Dan Quisenberry

"The Mets just had their first .500 or better April since July of 1992."
          -Broadcaster Ralph Kiner

"Don't know. They were wearing a bag over their head."
          -Yogi Berra, when asked if a "streaker" was
          male or female

"Scott Bullett, as he takes left field, is getting congratulations from everybody. He and his daughter are parents now of a new baby."
          -Chicago Cubs broadcaster Harry Caray

LAUGH-IN TIME-OUT
(CONTINUED)

"I want to thank all my players for giving me the honor of being what I was."
                                        -Casey Stengel

"Rich Folkers is throwing up in the bullpen."
                                        -Padres broadcaster Jerry Coleman

"The Mets have gotten their leadoff batter on base only once this inning."
                                        -Ralph Kiner

"I watch a lot of baseball on radio."
                                        -Former U.S. president Gerald R. Ford

"I don't know. I'm not in shape yet."
                                        -Yogi Berra, when asked about his cap size

"All the lies about him are true."
                                        -Joe Dugan, on his former teammate Babe Ruth

"Now there's three things you can do in a baseball game: you can win or you can lose or it can rain."
                                        -Casey Stengel

"My goals are to hit .300, score 100 runs, and stay injury prone."
                                        -Yankee outfielder Mickey Rivers

SECOND GUESSING

1. Pete Rose has played in the most games, 3,562. Who's second?

2. Of all the big leaguers whose last name begins with the letter "R," Babe Ruth tops the career home run list with 714. What slugger is second?

3. Of lefthanded batters, who's second to the Babe in career homers?

4. In 1998, what keystone sacker became only the second player in history to have had 50 doubles and 50 stolen bases in the same season?

5. What became the second home of the St. Louis Browns?

6. In 2001, Alex Rodriguez hit 52 home runs, the most ever by a shortstop. Who's second?

7. Roger Clemens began his career with the Red Sox. What was the second team he played for?

8. The Detroit Tigers first played their home games at Bennett Park. What stadium was their second home?

9. Mike Marshall of the Dodgers set the record for most games pitched in one season, 104, in 1974. What Pittsburgh reliever is second with 94 appearances?

10. Who's second to Lou Gehrig in career grand slams?

ANSWERS

1. Carl Yastrzemski, 3,308.

2. Frank Robinson, 586.

3. Barry Bonds.

4. Craig Biggio hit 51 doubles and stole 50 bases for the Astros. Tris Speaker of the 1912 Red Sox had 53 doubles and 52 steals.

5. Baltimore, where they became known as the Orioles.

6. Ernie Banks, 47.

7. The Blue Jays.

8. Tiger Stadium ... Comerica Park became their third home in 2000.

9. Kent Tekulve, 94.

10. Eddie Murray, with 19 grand slams was runner-up to Gehrig's 23.

INFIELD CHATTER

"If I only had a little humility, I'd be perfect."

- Ted Turner

BY ANY OTHER NAME

The following are not generally known by their given first names which are provided in the clues.

1. Walter was a pioneer broadcaster who did play by play for the Dodgers as well as the Yankees.

2. Lewis hit 56 home runs for the Cubs in 1930, a team record which stood until 1998 when Sammy Sosa hit 66.

3. Edward pitched for 16 years and won 236 games for the Yankees.

4. James was another hurler who won 224 games for the A's and Yankees.

5. Another James, he too a moundsman, led the American League in victories with a 21-7 record for the Minnesota Twins in 1965.

6. Harold was a longtime shortstop of the Dodgers, playing from 1940 to 1958 and participating in seven World Series.

7. Denton's 379th career victory was a perfect game.

8. Anthony was AL Rookie of the Year with the Red Sox.

9. Vincent was a Heisman Trophy winner, pro football running back and big league baseball player.

10. Richard was a relief pitcher for 18 years, the highlight of which was as the bullpen ace for the 1978 world champion Yankees.

ANSWERS

1. Red Barber.

2. Hack Wilson.

3. Whitey Ford.

4. Catfish Hunter.

5. Mudcat Grant.

6. Pee Wee Reese.

7. Cy Young.

8. Nomar Garciaparra.

9. Bo Jackson.

10. Goose Gossage.

INFIELD CHATTER

"Baseball is the only field of endeavor where a man can succeed three times out of ten and be considered a good performer."

- Ted Williams

THE FALL CLASSIC

1. What two teams participated in the first World Series played entirely on artificial turf?

2. Of all the players to have had at least 50 at bats in World Series play, what two men are tied with the highest average, .418? (Hint: Both of their initials are "P.M.")

3. What team had only nine batters go to the plate during an entire World Series?

4. What player hit the most home runs in a single World Series?

5. He played in the World Series with the same club in the '60s, '70s and '80s and was the youngest pitcher to hurl a complete game shutout. Name him.

6. Who delivered the winning hit for the Diamondbacks in the bottom of the ninth inning of Game Seven of the 2001 World Series?

7. What team has won the most consecutive Fall Classics ... And how many?

8. What player hit the first World Series home run in Yankee Stadium? (Hint: You know him better as a manager.)

9. Gene Tenace homered in his first two at bats for the A's in the 1972 World Series. What Braves rookie duplicated that feat in 1996?

10. What claim to fame does Bill Wambsganss hold?

ANSWERS

1. The Kansas City Royals and Philadelphia Phillies in 1980.

2. Pepper Martin and Paul Molitor.

3. The 1976 Cincinnati Reds (when the designated hitter rule was in effect) ... The hitters were Tony Perez, Joe Morgan, Dave Concepcion, Pete Rose, Johnny Bench, George Foster, Cesar Geronimo, Ken Griffey and Dan Driessen.

4. Reggie Jackson, 5 in the 1977 World Series (and three in one game).

5. Jim Palmer.

6. Luis Gonzalez.

7. The New York Yankees, 5 (from 1949-'53).

8. Casey Stengel, in 1923 ... In the first Series game ever played at the Stadium, Stengel hit a ninth-inning inside-the-park home run to give the Giants a win over the Yankees.

9. Andruw Jones.

10. He turned the World Series first unassisted triple play for the Indians against the Dodgers in 1920.

TRADING PLACES

1. The Phillies swapped a second baseman and a shortstop to the Cubs for Ivan DeJesus in 1982. Can you name either of them?

2. Following the 1956 season, the New York Giants made a deal with the Dodgers to trade pitcher Dick Littlefield, but it was killed when what Brooklyn player opted for retirement?

3. In 1964, pitcher Ernie Broglio was the primary player traded from the St. Louis Cardinals to the Chicago Cubs for what future base stealing star?

4. Brooklyn Dodgers g.m. Branch Rickey traded a minor league ball player to the Atlanta Crackers for an announcer in 1948. That man would later become a fixture in the Detroit Tigers broadcasting booth. Who is he?

5. Who, besides Joe De Maestri and Kent Hadley, did the Yankees get when they unloaded four players to the A's in 1959?

6. In a baseball first, the Cleveland Indians and Detroit Tigers traded managers in 1960. Who were they?

7. Do you know the only player to be traded after winning the Triple Crown?

8. What future four-time Cy Young Award winner was traded from the Cardinals to the Phillies for pitcher Rick Wise in 1972?

9. In 1965, Baltimore traded pitchers Milt Pappas and Jack Baldschun and outfielder Dick Simpson to Cincinnati for what slugger?

10. In 1962, the Cleveland Indians traded catcher Harry Chiti to the New York Mets for a player to be named later. Who became that player to be named later?

ANSWERS

1. Ryne Sandberg and Larry Bowa.

2. Jackie Robinson.

3. Lou Brock.

4. Ernie Harwell.

5. Roger Maris.

6. Joe Gordon and Jimmie Dykes.

7. Chuck Klein, in 1933 ... He went to the Cubs from the Phillies in exchange for Mark Koenig, Harvey Hendrick, Ted Kleinhans and $125,000.

8. Steve Carlton.

9. Frank Robinson.

10. Harry Chiti himself.

INFIELD CHATTER

"Im glad I don't play anymore.
I could never learn all those handshakes."

-Phil Rizzuto

DINGERS

1. Who hit four homers and tied Jim Bottomley's single game record of 12 RBI's in 1993?

2. Who's the only man to homer in his first two regular season at-bats?

3. What slugger set a record by homering from both sides of the plate in the same game four times in 1996?

4. Who holds the record for most homers leading off a game in one season?

5. Who were the only two players to hit a home run in the majors before their 20th and after their 40th birthdays?

6. Who hit the first home run in the Astrodome?

7. Who had the most at-bats in a season with no home runs?

8. What Oakland A's player is the only man to homer in his final career at-bats in both regular-season and World Series play?

9. Of all the players whose last name begins with the letter "K," who has had the most seasons of 40 homers or more?

10. What pitcher gave up the most home runs in a season? (Hint: He was a Minnesota Twin and the year was 1986.)

ANSWERS

1. Mark Whiten of the Cardinals, against the Reds.

2. Bob Nieman of the 1951 St. Louis Browns.

3. San Diego's Ken Caminiti.

4. Brady Anderson of the Orioles, 12 times in 1996.

5. Rusty Staub and Ty Cobb.

6. Mickey Mantle, in an exhibition game in 1965 ... Richie Allen was the first to homer in a regular season contest.

7. Pittsburgh's Rabbit Maranville, 672 at-bats in 1922.

8. Joe Rudi.

9. Harmon Killebrew, 8.

10. Bert Blyleven, 50.

INFIELD CHATTER

"When I am right, no one remembers.
When I am wrong, no one forgets."

-Umpire *Doug Harvey*

POTPOURRI

1. Who was the last big leaguer to turn an unassisted triple play?

2. Phillies great Mike Schmidt was voted starting NL third baseman for the '89 All-Star Game but didn't play. Why?

3. Two baseball Hall of Famers once played for the Harlem Globetrotters. Can you "pitch" us their names?

4. What record-setting star often avoided attention by registering at hotels under the alias George Ruth?

5. Who played in the most regular season baseball games without appearing in a post-season contest?

6. Two center fielders have won back-to-back MVPs, one in the AL and one in the NL. Can you name them?

7. What team has lost the most games in a season?

8. What's the name of the park where the annual Baseball Hall of Fame Game is played?

9. Willie Stargell and John Wehner hit the first and last homers at what ball park?

10. Who, in 2002, became the second Yankee, after Babe Ruth, to hit a walk-off grand slam while trailing by three runs?

ANSWERS

1. Randy Velarde of the A's, against the Yankees on Memorial Day, 2000.

2. He retired before the game.

3. Bob Gibson and Ferguson Jenkins.

4. Hank Aaron, who, of course, bested the Babe's all-time home run mark.

5. Ernie Banks, 2,528 games.

6. Mickey Mantle and Dale Murphy.

7. The 1962 New York Mets ... In their inaugural year, the hapless club was 40-120.

8. Abner Doubleday Field.

9. Three Rivers Stadium in Pittsburgh.

10. Jason Giambi ... His homer came in the 14th inning and gave New York a 13-12 win over the Twins.

INFIELD CHATTER

"Has anybody every satisfactorily explained why the bad hop is always the last one?"

Broadcaster *Hank Greenwald*

THE ALL-STAR GAME

1. Who was selected to play in the most All-Star Games?

2. What National League first baseman has the most All-Star Game home runs?

3. Who went 4-for-4, hit two homers and drove in five runs in his own park to lead the AL to a 12-0 rout over the NL in 1946?

4. What pitcher struck out five straight American Leaguers in the 1934 All-Star Game?

5. Who are the only two catchers from the same team to catch in one All-Star Game? Hint: The year was 1961.

6. The 2002 All-Star Game resulted in an 11-inning tie, 7-7, when baseball commissioner Bud Selig halted the contest because each league had used all of their pitchers. In what year was the only other tie and what was the reason for it?

7. In 1983, he hit the first grand slam ever in an All-Star Game, enroute to a 13-3 American League victory. Name him.

8. Here's a question for your baseball and history wits: Who, in 1937, became the first U.S. President to throw out the ceremonial first ball for the All-Star Game?

9. Who is Arch Ward?

10. What father-and-son combo were the first to win All-Star MVP awards?

ANSWERS

1. Hank Aaron, 25.

2. Stan Musial, 6.

3. Ted Williams.

4. Carl Hubbell ... He fanned Babe Ruth, Lou Gehrig, Jimmie Foxx, Al Simmons and Joe Cronin, in that order. Despite his performance, the AL won, 9-7.

5. Yogi Berra and Elston Howard of the Yankees.

6. In 1961, when the game was called because of rain, a 1-1 nine inning deadlock at Fenway Park in Boston.

7. Fred Lynn.

8. Franklin D. Roosevelt.

9. He's the Chicago Tribune sports editor who founded the All-Star Game in 1933 as the featured sports event of Chicago's Century of Progress Exposition.

10. Ken Griffey Sr and Ken Griffey Jr - Ken Sr for the NL in 1980 and Ken Jr for the AL in 1992.

ON THE JOHN

His first name is John. What's his last name?

1. He's the only man ever to homer in his first at bat and his last plate appearance.

2. He has more lifetime homers than any other catcher, 389.

3. This catcher was clubbed by Juan Marichal in a Giant-Dodger brawl.

4. A relief pitcher for the Yankees, he was the 1996 World Series MVP.

5. He's one of two managers to have won 10 pennants.

6. He hit 359 lifetime homers, including 51 with the 1947 New York Giants.

7. He played right field for the Phillies and hit a three-run homer in the ninth inning of the 1964 All-Star Game to give the NL a 7-4 win.

8. A shortstop for the Red Sox in the '40s and early '50s, he managed the club in '63 and '64 and, briefly, in '80.

9. He's the Mets' pitcher who surrendered Roberto Clemente's 3,000th and last regular-season major league hit. (Hint: His first name is spelled Jon.)

10. A big league infielder for 11 seasons, he played for the 1948 world champion Cleveland Indians and later played Dr. Steve Hardy on the television soap opera *General Hospital.*

ANSWERS

1. Miller ... He hit only two homers in his career, in his first at bat as a Yankee in 1966 and in his final at bat as a Dodger in 1969.

2. Bench.

3. Roseboro.

4. Wetteland.

5. McGraw ... The other is Casey Stengel.

6. Mize.

7. Callison.

8. Pesky.

9. Matlack.

10. Berardino.

INFIELD CHATTER

"When we lost, I couldn't sleep at night.
When we win, I can't sleep at night.
But when you win, you wake up feeling better."

-Joe Torre

MONIKERS

Identify the baseballer by the nickname.

1. The 'Ol Perfessor
2. Bullet Bob
3. The Big Hurt
4. Dr. Strangeglove
5. The Say Hey Kid
6. Teddy Ballgame
7. The Toy Cannon
8. The Fordham Flash
9. Big Six
10. Buy a Vowel

INFIELD CHATTER

"If a guy is a good fastball hitter,
does that mean I should throw him a bad fastball?"

-Larry Andersen

ANSWERS

1. Casey Stengel.

2. Bob Feller.

3. Frank Thomas.

4. Dick Stuart.

5. Willie Mays.

6. Ted Williams.

7. Jim Wynn.

8. Frankie Frisch.

9. Christy Mathewson.

10. Kent Hrbek.

INFIELD CHATTER

"The Good Lord was good to me.
He gave me a strong body, a good right arm
and a weak mind."

-*Dizzy Dean*

WHO YOU TALKIN' 'BOUT?

Below are ten quotes and the person quoted. Can you figure out the
baseball great each was talking about?

1. "They invented the All-Star Game for _____ _____." -Hall of
   Famer Ted Williams

2. "Trying to throw a fastball by _____ _____ is like trying to
   sneak the sunrise past a rooster." -Phillies pitcher Curt Simmons

3. "Having _____ _____ on your ballclub is like having a
   diamond ring on your finger." -Pirates manager Chuck Tanner

4. "On two legs, _____ _____ would have been the greatest
   ballplayer who ever lived." -White Sox second baseman
   Nellie Fox

5. "He's the greatest Jewish athlete since Samson." -Comedian
   Georgie Jessel

6. "The trick against _____ _____ is to hit him before he hits
   you." -Giants first baseman Orlando Cepeda

7. "While he did mangle a phrase now and then, with _____
   _____ it was important that you listen to what he was
   saying, not how; and what he said generally made very good
   sense." -Writer Donald Honig

8. "Every time I look at my pocket book, I see _____
   _____." -Hall of Famer Willie Mays

9. "No one hit home runs the way _____ _____ did. They were
   something special. They were like homing pigeons. The ball
   would leave the bat, pause briefly, suddenly gain its bearings,
   then take off for the stands." -Yankees pitcher Lefty Gomez

10. "We finished last with you. We can finish last without you."
    -Pirates general manager Branch Rickey

ANSWERS

1. Willie Mays.

2. Hank Aaron.

3. Willie Stargell.

4. Mickey Mantle.

5. Sandy Koufax.

6. Don Drysdale.

7. Casey Stengel.

8. Jackie Robinson.

9. Babe Ruth.

10. Ralph Kiner (during contract negotiations).

INFIELD CHATTER

"The reason baseball calls itself a game,
I believe, is that it is too screwed up to be a business."

-Jim Bouton

RHYME TIME

Try your hand at these poetic puzzlers.

1. The 1948 Boston Braves had a mediocre pitching staff with the exception of Warren Spahn and Johnny Sain. As a result what short rhyme became well known?

2. Who wrote *Baseball's Saddest Lexicon* (the tribute to the Tinker to Evers to Chance double play trio)?

3. What's the first line of the poem?

4. What team was the double play combo on?

5. What were the first names of Tinker, Evers and Chance?

6. Who was Harry Steinfeldt?

7. What song, written in 1908, had words by Jack Norworth and music by Harry von Tilzer?

8. Who penned *Casey at the Bat*?

9. How many people were at that game in Mudville?

10. What was the final line of the poem?

ANSWERS

1. "Spahn and Sain and pray for rain."

2. Franklin Pierce Adams.

3. "These are the saddest of possible words..."

4. The Chicago Cubs.

5. Joe, Johnny and Frank.

6. He was the third baseman on the team.

7. *Take Me Out to the Ball Game.* (At the time they wrote it, neither one had ever seen a baseball game.)

8. Ernest Lawrence Thayer, in 1888.

9. 5,000 ("Ten thousand eyes were on him...")

10. "But there is no joy in Mudville - mighty Casey has struck out."

INFIELD CHATTER

A complete ballplayer today is one who can hit, field, run, throw and pick the right agent.

-Bob Lurie

FACT OR FIB?

1. The Washington Senators forfeited their final game ever.

2. Dennis Eckersley has pitched in more games than anyone else in baseball history.

3. Before 1900, foul balls were not counted as strikes.

4. New York Yankees catcher Elston Howard invented the batting donut.

5. John F. Kennedy was the first president to throw out the ceremonial Opening Day first ball.

6. Eric Gregg was the first African-American major league baseball umpire.

7. Hank Aaron was a designated hitter when he hit his last home run.

8. Bob Gibson was the last National League pitcher to win at least 30 games in a season.

9. During World War II, American soldiers in their foxholes would shout out indignities about Emperor Hirohito to their Japanese enemies. Revengefully, the Japanese frequently shouted out, "To hell with Babe Ruth!"

10. When Charles O. Finley owned the A's, he bought a mascot - a mule he named Charlie O.

ANSWERS

1. Fact ... On September 30, 1971, the Senators were leading the Yankees 7-5 with two out in the ninth when souvenir hungry fans swarmed the field and the game could not be resumed.

2. Fib ... Jesse Orosco owns that mark.

3. Fact.

4. Fact.

5. Fib ... It was William Howard Taft, in 1910.

6. Fib ... It was Emmett Ashford, in 1966.

7. Fact ... He was playing for the Milwaukee Brewers, then in the AL, at the time.

8. Fib ... Dizzy Dean was the last NL hurler to win 30, in 1934 when he was 30-7.

9. Fact.

10. Fact.

INFIELD CHATTER

"I've always said that a home run is a baseball that just goes over the fence."

-Mark McGwire

ALPHABET SOUP

1. Of all major league managers whose last name begins with the letter "A," who has won the most pennants?

2. Unless you're a baby boomer baseball buff, you'll have a tough time with this one: What 1960s pitcher had a four-letter last name which began with three consonants?

3. If baseball's Hall of Famers were listed in alphabetical order, whose name would be last?

4. Can you name the baseball commissioner whose first and last initials were the same?

5. In a 1980 game against the Tigers, the Kansas City Royals formed baseball's first "Q" battery. Jamie Quirk was the catcher. Who was the pitcher?

6. Who was known as "Double X?"

7. J.R. Richard won more than 100 games for the Houston Astros before an injury curtailed his career in 1980. Do you know what his initials stand for?

8. What pitcher was referred to as "Dr. K?"

9. What does "KS" mean on a baseball scorecard?

10. "H" as in homer: There have been two players whose last names begin with the letter "H" who've homered four times in a single game. Who are they?

ANSWERS

1. Walter Alston, seven.

2. Eli Grba.

3. Robin Yount.

4. Ford Frick.

5. Dan Quisenberry.

6. Jimmie Foxx.

7. James Rodney.

8. Dwight Gooden.

9. Strikeout swinging.

10. Gil Hodges and Bob Horner.

INFIELD CHATTER

If horses won't eat it (artificial turf),
I don't want to play on it.

Dick Allen

THE TROPHY CASE

1. In 1979, two players shared the NL MVP award. Who were they?

2. What World Series MVP is married to to an LPGA Hall of Famer?

3. Name the third sacker who won 16 Gold Glove awards.

4. Who won both the AL Rookie of the Year and MVP awards in 2001?

5. Who has won the most Cy Young Awards?

6. He was the NL Cy Young and MVP winner in 1963, the NL Cy Young winner in '65 and the first player to win the World Series MVP award twice. Who is he?

7. Who's the last pitcher to win an MVP award?

8. In 1999 and 2000, two pitchers won back-to-back Cy Young awards in the American and National Leagues. Name them.

9. There have been three players whose initials are "T.S." that have won Rookie of the Year awards. Two are in the National League (in 1967 and '69) and one in the junior circuit (1993). Do you know them?

10. Here's one to throw you off: The AL MVP of 1953 was a third baseman from the Cleveland Indians. Can you name him, and for extra special credit, do you know why he's only 23 years old today?

ANSWERS

1. Keith Hernandez and Willie Stargell.

2. Ray Knight, who won the MVP in 1986, is the husband of Nancy Lopez.

3. Brooks Robinson.

4. Ichiro Suzuki.

5. Roger Clemens, six.

6. Sandy Koufax.

7. Dennis Eckersley, in 1992.

8. Pedro Martinez (AL) and Randy Johnson (NL).

9. Tom Seaver and Ted Sizemore of the NL and the AL's Tim Salmon.

10. Al Rosen ... He was born February 29, 1924 so his birthday is celebrated only once every four years.

INFIELD CHATTER

"Slumps are like a soft bed.
They're easy to get into and hard to get out of."

-Johnny Bench

NAMES AND NUMBERS

1. Do you know the player who wore his birth date on the back of his uniform?

2. What number did Babe Ruth wear when he hit his 60th home run in 1927?

3. In 1970, Detroit Tigers' shortstop Cesar Gutierrez became the first player to get seven hits in seven at bats in a game. What was his uniform number?

4. What number did pitcher Ralph Branca wear when he served up the "shot heard 'round the world," the Bobby Thomson homer in 1951 which gave the Giants the pennant over the Dodgers?

5. Hank Aaron wore uniform number 44 when he hit his record-breaking 715th home run off Dodgers hurler Al Downing. What number was Downing wearing?

6. When pitcher Bill Voiselle was obtained by the Boston Braves in 1947 he was given the number 96. Any idea why?

7. The number 29 has been retired by two teams. For whom?

8. The Angels retired uniform number 26 in honor of their "26th man". Who was that?

9. Who wore uniform number seven on the New York Yankees before Mickey Mantle?

10. The uniform number of baseball comedian Max Patkin was ?

ANSWERS

1. Carlos May. The back of his jersey had his last name and the number 17. He was born May 17, 1948, in Birmingham, Alabama.

2. He didn't have one ... Uniform numbers were not introduced until 1929.

3. Seven.

4. 13 ... He changed his number to 12 the following year.

5. He, ironically, also wore number 44. (After giving up number 715 to Aaron, Downing remarked, "I never say 'seven-fifteen' anymore. I now say 'quarter after seven.'")

6. Voiselle was from the town of Ninety Six, South Carolina.

7. Rod Carew ... Both the Twins and Angels retired it for him.

8. Owner Gene Autry.

9. Cliff Mapes.

10. Hope you didn't fall for this one ... That was not a question, it was a statement. Patkin wore a question mark on the back of his uniform.

MULTIPLE CHOICE

1. The son of what Cy Young Award winner for baseball has won more than a million dollars on golf's PGA tour?
   a) Jim Perry b) Sandy Koufax c) Nolan Ryan d) Meg Ryan

2. What player has walked the most times in his career? a) Babe Ruth b) Ty Cobb c) Rickey Henderson d) Florence Henderson

3. Who's the only person to hit a major league home run and score an NFL touchdown in the same week? a) Jim Thorpe b) Deion Sanders c) Bo Jackson d) Michael Jackson

4. Three men have won MVP and Manager of the Year Awards. Two are Don Baylor and Joe Torre. Who's the third?
   a) Billy Martin b) Harvey Kuenn c) Frank Robinson
   d) Smokey Robinson

5. Who was the last man to steal 100 bases in a season? a) Lou Brock b) Maury Wills c) Vince Coleman d) Gary Coleman

6. Who was the first player ever to hit 400 homers and amass 3,000 hits? a) Stan Musial b) Babe Ruth c) Ted Williams d) Hank Williams

7. What future Manager of the Year lost 24 games as a pitcher for the Mets in 1962? a) Roger Craig b) Bob Lemon c) Dallas Green d) Tom Green

8. Who hit the most home runs in the decade of the '90s?
   a) Barry Bonds b) Mark McGwire c) Eddie Murray
   d) Bill Murray

9. What baseball Rookie of the Year played his entire 19-year career with one team? a) Lou Whitaker b) Luis Aparicio c) Richie Allen d) Steve Allen

10. Who was the first African-American to pitch in a World Series? a) Joe Black b) Satchel Paige c) Bob Gibson d) Mel Gibson

ANSWERS

1. A ... His son is Chris Perry.

2. C.

3. B, in 1989.

4. C.

5. C ... He pilfered 109 bases in 1987.

6. A.

7. A.

8. B, 405.

9. A (with the Detroit Tigers).

10. B.

INFIELD CHATTER

"Man, if I made one million dollars, I would be in at 6 in the morning, sweep the stands, wash the uniforms, clean out the office, manage the team and play the game."

-Hall of Famer *Duke Snider*

TAKE ME OUT TO THE OLD BALLPARK

Name these extinct stadiums.

1. Located in Washington D.C., it was the site of a 565-foot Mickey Mantle home run.

2. A domed stadium, it was imploded in the year 2000 despite 208 million dollars still mortgaged on it.

3. "Disco Demolition Derby Night" proved to be a fiasco and a forfeiture for the home team in this park after thousands of fans hurled discos all over the field.

4. The Montreal Expos played their first home games there.

5. On July 31, 1954, Braves first baseman Joe Adcock hit four home runs in this stadium as Milwaukee romped over the Dodgers, 15-7.

6. It was home to the Athletics from 1909-1954 and to the Phillies from 1938-1970.

7. On October 9, 1916, Babe Ruth pitched the Red Sox to a 14-inning, 2-1 win over the Dodgers in the second game of the World Series at this ballpark.

8. It was labeled "The mistake by the lake."

9. On May 26,1959, Harvey Haddix of the Pirates pitched 12 perfect innings but lost to the Braves 1-0 in the 13th at this stadium.

10. It was the site of Greenberg Gardens - later known as Kiner's Korner.

ANSWERS

1. Griffith Stadium.

2. Seattle's Kingdome.

3. Comiskey Park (the old one), home of the Chicago White Sox.

4. Jarry Park.

5. Ebbets Field.

6. Connie Mack Stadium.

7. Braves Field. (In 1915 and 1916 the Red Sox played their World Series home games there.)

8. Cleveland's Municipal Stadium.

9. Milwaukee County Stadium.

10. Forbes Field.

INFIELD CHATTER

"Statistics are used like a drunk uses a lamp post -
for support, not illumination."

- Vin Scully

LAUGH-IN TIME-OUT

Okay, it's the seventh inning stretch - time for a round of groaners before stepping up to the plate for the final rounds of trivia.

Did you hear about the pitcher and his expectant wife?
They both suffered from complete exhaustion in the ninth.

They've just invented a microwave television.
Now you can watch a three hour baseball game in four minutes.

Q: What's the difference between a baseball and Prince Charles?
A: One's thrown to the air, the other heir to the throne.

Pitcher: I thought I had pretty good stuff today.
Manager: The guys on the other team sure liked it.

Q: How many baseball broadcasters does it take to change a light bulb?
A: Two ... one to change it and one to do the color.

Q: What's the difference between an umpire and a pickpocket?
A: An umpire watches steals, a pickpocket steals watches.

Q: If a basketball team was running after a baseball team, what time would it be?
A: Five after nine.

Did you hear about the dentist who was an avid baseball fan?
During the day he yanked at roots and at night he rooted for the Yanks.

LAUGH-IN TIME-OUT
(CONTINUED)

Q: What do a musical conductor and a baseball statistician have in common?
A: They both know the score.

Q: How do you make a slow baserunner fast?
A: Don't feed him.

Then there was the Cleveland baseball player who wouldn't sign his contract.
He was a wouldn't Indian.

Mrs. Jones was giving her third-grade class a geography lesson.
"Can anyone tell me where Baltimore is?" she asked the class.
Little Johnny raised his hand.
"Yes, Johnny."
"Baltimore is at Cleveland today."

Q: Why did they stop selling beer at the doubleheader?
A: Because the home team lost the opener.

The diehard fan told his friend, "I've gotta cut down on hot dogs and beer."
"How come?"
"Because I'm starting to get a ballpark figure."

Player #1: "How'd you make out with the owner's daughter?
Player #2: "Horrible ... no hits, no runs, no heiress.

Q: Where did they put the matador who joined the baseball club?
A: In the bullpen.

THE FIFTIES

1. What National Leaguer won three straight batting crowns in the '50s?

2. In 1951, he became the first American League pitcher to record two no-hitters in a season. Name him.

3. What slugger hit the most homers during the 1950s?

4. The first Cy Young Award was won by what pitcher in 1956?

5. Who was a pitcher on the 1957 world champion Milwaukee Braves and also a member of the NBA champion Boston Celtics in 1959, 1960 and 1961?

6. Two catchers from the AL and NL were selected MVPs in both 1951 and 1955. Who were they?

7. What National League team won the most pennants in the '50s?

8. Who led the American League in batting with a .388 average in 1957?

9. Who made the final out in Don Larsen's 1956 World Series perfect game?

10. Name the man who was on deck when Bobby Thomson hit the three run homer to give the Giants the pennant over the Dodgers in 1951.

ANSWERS

1. Stan Musial, in 1950, '5l and '52.

2. Allie Reynolds.

3. Duke Snider, 326.

4. Don Newcombe of the Dodgers ... He also won the National League MVP award that year.

5. Gene Conley.

6. Yogi Berra and Roy Campanella.

7. The Dodgers, five.

8. Ted Williams.

9. Dale Mitchell.

10. Willie Mays.

INFIELD CHATTER

"Us ballplayers do things backwards.
First we play, then we retire and go to work."

-*Charlie Gehringer*

THE SIXTIES

1. Sandy Koufax and Juan Marichal were two of the best pitchers during this decade. With what teams did they end their careers?

2. Who hit four homers in a 14-4 Giants win over the Braves on April 30, 1961?

3. The Dodgers swept and were swept in the World Series during the '60s. Can you name their opponents?

4. Who was the World Series MVP in 1960 even though he wasn't on the winning team?

5. Two men won all the NL stolen base crowns during the '60s, one from 1960-'65, the other from 1966-'69. Who were they?

6. What American Leaguer won back-to-back MVP awards in the '60s?

7. What rookie won the American League batting title in 1964?

8. What NL Cy Young Award winner posted a record of 22-9 with 13 shutouts and a 1.12 ERA in 1968?

9. The 1965 L.A. Dodgers featured the big league's first all-switch hitting infield. How many of the four do you know?

10. He was the victim of Bill Mazeroski's 1960 World Series winning home run and then redeemed himself with a 1-0 seventh game victory over the Giants in 1962. Name him.

ANSWERS

1. Both ended their careers with the Dodgers.

2. Willie Mays.

3. They defeated the Yankees in four straight in 1963 and were swept by the Orioles in 1966.

4. Bobby Richardson of the Yankees, who were beaten by the Pirates in seven games.

5. Maury Wills and Lou Brock.

6. Roger Maris, in 1960 and '61.

7. Tony Oliva.

8. Bob Gibson.

9. Wes Parker played first base, Jim Lefebvre was at second, Maury Wills at short and Jim Gilliam at third.

10. Ralph Terry of the Yankees.

INFIELD CHATTER

"Umpiring is best described as the profession of standing between two 7-year olds with one ice cream cone."

-Ron Luciano

THE SEVENTIES

1. What team won the most World Series in the 1970s?

2. How about the club that lost the most Fall Classics during the decade?

3. How many All-Star Games did the American League win in the '70s?

4. What slugger hit the most homers for this decade?

5. What pitcher won 27 games for a last place team in 1972?

6. When Hank Aaron hit home run number 715 to break Babe Ruth's record in 1974, what relief pitcher caught the ball after it went over the fence?

7. Who's the only catcher to win a home run title?

8. He won the Cy Young Award in both leagues, with the Indians in 1972 and with the Padres in 1978. Name him.

9. Who won back-to-back MVP awards in the National League in 1975 and 1976?

10. Who earned the nickname "Mr. October" for his World Series performances during the '70s?

ANSWERS

1. The Oakland A's, who won three straight from 1972-'74.

2. The L.A. Dodgers, who were losers to the A's in '74 and to the Yankees in '77 and '78.

3. Just one, in 1971 (6-4 over the NL). In fact, from 1960 to 1982, 25 All-Star Games were played and the American League won only two.

4. Willie Stargell, 296.

5. Steve Carlton of the Phillies.

6. Tom House.

7. Johnny Bench, in 1970 and '72.

8. Gaylord Perry.

9. Joe Morgan of the Cincinnati Reds.

10. Reggie Jackson.

INFIELD CHATTER

"Ninety feet between the bases is the nearest thing to perfection that man has yet achieved."

-Sportswriter *Red Smith*

THE EIGHTIES

1. What rookie manager won the World Series in 1987?

2. In 1986, '87 and '88, the Rookie of the Year Award was won by members of the Oakland A's. How many do you know?

3. Pete Rose got his 4,000th hit while playing with what team in 1984?

4. What Hall of Fame shortstop/outfielder had the most hits during the decade of the '80s?

5. Who stole a record 130 bases in 1982?

6. Name the politician and former Cubs radio broadcaster who returned to the booth (TV this time) to do an inning at the 1989 All-Star Game.

7. What Detroit pitcher, with 162 wins, had the most victories in the '80s?

8. Do you know the hurler who gave up George Brett's "pine tar" homer in 1983?

9. Who had the most homers in the '80s?

10. Who won three MVP awards during the '80s?

ANSWERS

1. Tom Kelly of the Minnesota Twins.

2. Jose Canseco, 1986; Mark McGwire, 1987; Walt Weiss, 1988.

3. The Montreal Expos.

4. Robin Yount, 1,731.

5. Rickey Henderson.

6. Ronald Reagan.

7. Jack Morris.

8. Goose Gossage.

9. Mike Schmidt, 313.

10. Again, Mike Schmidt.

INFIELD CHATTER

"The last time the Cubs won the World Series was 1908.
The last time they were in one was 1945.
Hey, any team can have a bad century."

-Cubs manager *Tom Trebelhorn*

THE NINETIES

1. Who resigned as Commissioner of Baseball in 1992?

2. What team played in the most World Series in the '90s?

3. What American League first baseman won back-to-back MVP awards in 1993 and 1994?

4. Name the pitcher who won four straight Cy Young Awards during the '90s.

5. For five consecutive years, from 1992 to 1996, a Los Angeles Dodger won the Rookie of the Year award. How many can you name?

6. The New York Yankees won three of the last four World Series of the 1900s. Who won the other one?

7. Do you know the only father and son to each have three-homer games?

8. With what team did Nolan Ryan win his 300th game?

9. In 1999, two Devil Rays teammates became the first to each hit 30 homers for four different teams. Who are they?

10. Who became the first player to hit 60 homers in back-to-back seasons?

ANSWERS

1. Faye Vincent.

2. The Atlanta Braves, five times (winning only once, in 1995).

3. Frank Thomas.

4. Greg Maddux, 1992-'95.

5. Eric Karros, Mike Piazza, Raul Mondesi, Hideo Nomo and Todd Hollandsworth.

6. The Florida Marlins, in 1997.

7. Ken Griffey Sr. (1986) and Jr. (1996).

8. The Rangers, in 1990.

9. Jose Canseco, who did it previously with the A's, Rangers and Blue Jays and Fred McGriff who did it with the Blue Jays, Padres and Braves.

10. Sammy Sosa, in 1998 and '99.

INFIELD CHATTER

"On Father's Day, we again wish you all happy birthday."

-Hall of Famer turned broadcaster **Ralph Kiner**

Y2K AND BEYOND

1. What pitcher was the victim of Barry Bonds' 73rd homer in 2001?

2. Name the 2001 team which set the record for most days in first place in a season.

3. Do you know the Yankee pitcher who, in 2000, tied the record for most strikeouts in a World Series game?

4. What do Keith McDonald, Chris Richard and Gene Stechschulte share in common besides being members of the St. Louis Cardinals?

5. On October 1, 2000, the Pirates played their final game at what stadium?

6. What player on the Detroit Tigers became only the fourth man in big league history to play all nine positions in one game?

7. What former Texas Rangers owner tossed out a ceremonial pitch before a game of the 2001 World Series between the Yankees and Diamondbacks?

8. Name the pitcher who went 3-0 in the 2001 World Series and was co-named *Sports Illustrated*'s Sportsman of the Year.

9. Who was named the 2001 All-Star Game MVP played at Safeco Field? Hint: He retired at the end of the season.

10. What's the name of the Cincinnati Reds' ballpark which was constructed in this decade?

ANSWERS

1. Dennis Springer of the Dodgers.

2. The Mariners, who won a total of 116 games, were in first place for 184 days.

3. Roger Clemens, 15.

4. All homered in their first big league at bat - McDonald and Richard in 2000 and Stechschulte in 2001.

5. Three Rivers Stadium ... Pittsburgh lost to the Cubs, 10-9.

6. Shane Halter, on the final day of the 2000 season.

7. President George W. Bush.

8. Randy Johnson ... Pitching mate Curt Schilling was his Sportsman of the Year partner.

9. Cal Ripken, Jr., ... In the game, he homered on the first pitch he saw from Chan Ho Park.

10. The Great American Ballpark.

INFIELD CHATTER

"If God let you hit a home run last time up,
then who struck you out the time before that?"

-Sparky Anderson

MISCELLANEOUS MINDBENDERS

1. The Milwaukee Brewers were formerly known as what team?

2. Ted Danson played what fictional retired pitcher for the Boston Red Sox in the hit television series *Cheers*?

3. How many Cy Young Awards did Nolan Ryan win?

4. Who's the only man to pinch-hit for Ted Williams?

5. Name the four 20-game winners for the 1971 Orioles.

6. What is the traditional "Flying of the flags" at Chicago's Wrigley Field?

7. What *Time* magazine Man of the Year managed a major league baseball team?

8. Of all the players whose last name begins with the letter "G," who has the highest lifetime batting average?

9. Who was the youngest player ever in the big leagues?

10. Which club did Sammy Sosa make his debut with in 1989?

ANSWERS

1. The Seattle Pilots.

2. Sam Malone.

3. None.

4. Carroll Hardy.

5. Jim Palmer, Dave McNally, Mike Cuellar and Pat Dobson.

6. After each game, a flag flies from the tall center field flagpole - a white one with a blue "W" to proclaim a Cubs win or a blue flag with a white "L" to announce a loss.

7. Ted Turner, owner of the Atlanta Braves ... He managed one game.

8. Lou Gehrig, .340. (Tony Gwynn's right behind him with a .338 mark.)

9. Joe Nuxhall of the Reds, who was 15 years, 10 months and 11 days old when he made his debut in 1944.

10. The Texas Rangers.

HALL OF FAME NAMES

Identify the Hall of Famer by his nickname.

1. Hammerin' Hank

2. The Commerce Comet

3. The Flying Dutchman

4. Mr. Sunshine

5. The Rajah

6. Tom Terrific

7. Wee Willie

8. The Wizard of Oz

9. Big Six

10. The Meal Ticket

INFIELD CHATTER

"I have an Alka-Seltzer bat. You know - plop, plop, fizz, fizz.
When the pitcher sees me walking up there he says,
'Oh, what a relief it is.'"

-Andy Van Slyke

ANSWERS

1. Henry Aaron.

2. Mickey Mantle.

3. Honus Wagner.

4. Ernie Banks, also known as Mr. Cub.

5. Rogers Hornsby.

6. Tom Seaver.

7. Willie Keeler.

8. Ozzie Smith.

9. Christy Mathewson.

10. Carl Hubbell.

HEADLINE/DATELINE

Match the year with the event.

1. 1924	a) Kiner Wins 7th Straight HR Title
2. 1941	b) Musial Retires
3. 1947	c) Oriole Park at Camden Yards Opens
4. 1952	d) Yanks Win Third Straight Series
5. 1958	e) Devil Rays and D'backs Debut
6. 1963	f) Dodgers and Giants Move to West Coast
7. 1969	g) Hornsby's .424 Sets Batting Record
8. 1992	h) Miracle Mets Win Fall Classic
9. 1998	i) Robinson Breaks Color Barrier
10. 2000	j) Dimaggio Hits in 56 Straight Games

INFIELD CHATTER

"I made a major contribution to the Cardinals
pennant drive in 1964. I got hepatitis."

-Bob Uecker

ANSWERS

1. G.

2. J.

3. I.

4. A.

5. F.

6. B. (Coincidentally, Musial finished up his career with 1,815 hits at home and 1,815 on the road.)

7. H.

8. C.

9. E.

10. D.

INFIELD CHATTER

"When my wife was sick, I took care of her.
I was a regular Florence Nightinguy."

- Yogi Berra

BATTERY MATES

*Listed below ae the last names of pitcher-catcher combos. The
letters are in their proper order, but the names have been combined.
See if you can flush out the hurler and backstop.*

Example - FOBRERDRA = Ford and Berra

1. CMARcLCATRVOERN

2. GBULELNECTH

3. PEPOTSTIATEDA

4. MALODPDUEXZ

5. KOROSUEBFOAXRO

6. SEGARVEOTRE

7. PROADRIRGUKEZ

8. MAVRATRIITNEEKZ

9. PDEAMLMPESERY

10. HTEUNNTAECRE

ANSWERS

1. Carlton and McCarver.

2. Gullet and Bench.

3. Pettite and Posada.

4. Maddux and Lopez.

5. Koufax and Roseboro.

6. Seaver and Grote.

7. Park and Rodriguez.

8. Martinez and Varitek.

9. Palmer and Dempsey.

10. Hunter and Tenace.

INFIELD CHATTER

"To compare baseball with other team games is to say the Hope Diamond is a nice chunk of carbon. The endless variety of physical and mental skills demanded by baseball is both uncomparable and incomparable."

-Bill Veeck

A MAN FOR ALL SEASONS

1. Who's the only man to play in a World Series, win an Olympic Gold Medal and be elected to the Pro Football Hall of Fame?

2. A football tackle from Syracuse, he was drafted by the Lions in 1959, but became a major league umpire after a knee injury curtailed his gridiron career. Who is he?

3. Who's the only man in the Baseball, Pro Football and College Football Halls of Fame?

4. Name the man who was a major league umpire, an NFL halfback and a pro basketball coach.

5. Who played parts of three seasons with the Blue Jays but had more success with the Boston Celtics and later became an NBA coach?

6. Who was captain of the University of Illinois basketball team in 1936-'37, but wound up having a Hall of Fame baseball career as a player/manager?

7. He won the MVP in 1960 while on the world champion Pirates and, earlier, was an All-America basketball star at Duke who played briefly for the NBA's Pistons. Name him.

8. What baseball Hall of Famer and former University of Minnesota basketballer was drafted by the NBA and ABA?

9. Who played for Atlanta's pro baseball and pro football teams for two seasons in the early '90s?

10. Who was the first man to play in a World Series and a Rose Bowl? (Hint: He played in the Rose Bowl with the 1949 California Golden Bears and in the World Series with the 1950 Yankees although his baseball career was primarily spent with the Boston Red Sox.)

ANSWERS

1. Jim Thorpe.

2. Ron Luciano.

3. Cal Hubbard.

4. Hank Soar ... He was an AL ump from 1950 to '71, played for the football Giants from 1937 to '44 and also in '46, and coached basketball's Providence Steamrollers in 1947 and '48.

5. Danny Ainge.

6. Lou Boudreau.

7. Dick Groat.

8. Dave Winfield.

9. Deion Sanders.

10. Jackie Jensen.

INFIELD CHATTER

"Putting lights in Wrigley Field is like putting aluminum siding on the Sistine Chapel."

-Columnist *Roger Simon*

ALL IN THE FAMILY

1. The father is the voice of the Atlanta Braves; the son does play-by-play for the Chicago Cubs. And they are?

2. What brothers combined for the most career pitching victories?

3. Name the pair of brothers who both hit safely in more than 30 consecutive games.

4. Do you know the only father-son combination to play in perfect games in the big leagues?

5. The last brother battery in baseball history teamed up for the Dodgers against the Mets in 1962. The pitcher was Larry, the catcher Norm. What's their last name?

6. Who's the only man in big league history to manage a father and son in the same season?

7. The father played for the New York Yankees for 19 years; the son played two seasons with the Bronx Bombers. Who are they?

8. What Boston Red Sox brother combination, in 1970, hit the most home runs in a major league season as teammates?

9. Who are the only brothers to finish 1-2 in a major league batting race? (Hint: The year was 1966.)

10. This one might ring a "bell": Who were the first father and son to appear in an All-Star Game, albeit separately?

ANSWERS

1. Skip and Chip Caray.

2. Phil and Joe Niekro ... Phil won 318 games and Joe won 221 for a total of 539.

3. Joe, 56 in 1941 and Dom Dimaggio, 34 in '49.

4. Dick Schofield and Dick Schofield, Jr. ... The father played in Pittsburgh hurler Harvey Haddix' perfect game in 1959 and the younger Schofield played shortstop when Mike Witt of the Angels went unblemished against the Rangers in 1984.

5. Sherry ... the Dodgers won the game, 5-4, in 13 innings.

6. Jim Lefebvre, who managed the 1990 and '91 Mariner teams that included Ken Griffey and Ken Griffey, Jr.

7. Yogi and Dale Berra.

8. Billy and Tony Conigliaro ... Tony hit 36, Billy 18.

9. Matty and Felipe Alou ... Matty won the NL batting championship, hitting .342 for the Pirates while Felipe came in second, batting .327 for the Braves.

10. Gus and Buddy Bell ... Gus played for the NL in 1953, '54, '56 and '57 games representing the Reds and Buddy played on the 1973 AL team as a member of the Indians and then in All-Star Games in 1980, '81, '82 and '84 while on the Rangers.

LAST CALL

With what team did these players wind up their careers?

1. Robin Roberts

2. Babe Ruth

3. Warren Spahn

4. Harmon Killebrew

5. Eddie Murray

6. Eddie Mathews

7. Willie Mays

8. Roger Maris

9. Steve Carlton

10. John Kruk

INFIELD CHATTER

"The secret of managing a club is to keep the five guys who hate you from the five who are undecided."

-Casey Stengel

ANSWERS

1. Chicago Cubs.

2. Boston Braves.

3. San Francisco Giants.

4. Kansas City Royals.

5. Los Angeles Dodgers.

6. Detroit Tigers.

7. New York Mets.

8. St. Louis Cardinals.

9. Minnesota Twins.

10. Chicago White Sox.

INFIELD CHATTER

"Even Napoleon had his Watergate."

-Phillies manager *Danny Ozark*

BOWL GAMES

Here's one last pitch as we invite you to take this toilet trivia test.

1. What manufacturer of a men's bathroom product once sponsored the All-Star Game balloting?

2. The last name of the winner of the 1986 NL Cy Young Award is the same as the name of a toilet paper maker. Do you know him?

3. What John has pitched in Cleveland, Chicago, Los Angeles, New York, Anaheim and Oakland?

4. What baseball team plays its home games in Flushing?

5. What former Brooklyn Dodger teamed up with Bob Cousy to form one of the most potent backcourts in NBA history? Hint: Think "Simply Charmin."

6. What former Baltimore designated hitter, whose initials are "J.L.," explained how he stays ready on the bench by saying, "I flush the john between innings to keep my wrists strong."

7. Name the Yankee third sacker who made this comment while on a plane trip: "We've got a problem. Luis Tiant wants to use the bathroom and it says no foreign objects in the toilet."

8. What NL stadium was manager Whitey Herzog referring to when he said, "It always did look like a toilet bowl. Now it has a seat on it?"

9. Give or take ten, how many bathrooms does Pro Player Stadium, home of the Marlins, have?

10. What former Dodger manager, famous for his locker room speeches, was known as the "porcelain preacher?"

ANSWERS

1. Gillette.

2. Mike Scott.

3. Tommy John.

4. The Mets ... Flushing is a section of Queens, one of the five boroughs of New York City.

5. It may be stretching the tissue ... err, issue, but his last name is pronounced the same as the toilet paper - Bill Sharman.

6. John Lowenstein.

7. Graig Nettles.

8. Olympic Stadium ... Herzog was talking about the new roof at the time.

9. 80 ... 40 men and 40 women's restrooms.

10. Tommy Lasorda.